A MAP

for the

MIDDLE

A MAP
—— *for the* ——
MIDDLE

MATTHEW SINK

AMBASSADOR INTERNATIONAL
GREENVILLE, SOUTH CAROLINA & BELFAST, NORTHERN IRELAND

www.ambassador-international.com

A Map for the Middle

Printed in the United States of America

Some names and identifying details have been changed to protect the privacy of individuals.

ISBN: 978-1-62020-238-8
eISBN: 978-1-62020-337-8

Cover design and typesetting: Matthew Mulder
E-book conversion: Anna Riebe

AMBASSADOR INTERNATIONAL
Emerald House
427 Wade Hampton Blvd.
Greenville, SC 29609, USA
www.ambassador-international.com

AMBASSADOR BOOKS
The Mount
2 Woodstock Link
Belfast, BT6 8DD, Northern Ireland, UK
www.ambassadormedia.co.uk

The colophon is a trademark of Ambassador

To Tonya, Jansen, Elissa, and Emmaline.

Thanks for your patience and support.

I love you.

TABLE OF CONTENTS

DEAR READER,

AS YOU CONTINUE TO GROW older, I guess you probably think we parents make a bigger deal out of things than necessary. Try for a moment, however, to see life through our eyes. We were there the day you were born. We're the ones who cut the cord and took you—a squirming, red-faced baby—and held you tightly.

You were tiny—more fragile than we imagined. We vowed to do whatever was required to protect you as you grew. We're your parents. That's our job.

For more than a decade, we have taken our job seriously. When you were learning to walk, we stood behind you and tried to keep you from getting hurt if you fell.

The first time you slid down the sliding board at the park, we were waiting at the bottom to catch you. When you insisted on swimming in deeper water, we walked behind you, prepared to grab you if you got in trouble.

This has been the theme throughout the years: you reach to try something new, and we parents try hard to keep you safe as you explore. I guess that's the natural relationship between parents and young children.

This dynamic won't change, now, as you enter middle school. We're still behind you, and we still want to protect you. The truth is, however, as hard as this is for me to accept, you have a bigger part to play in how things happen over these next seven years.

The decisions you make in middle and high school are critical ones in setting the direction of your life. Some decisions you'll make when we're not looking. We can't follow you around anymore to make sure you stay balanced.

Increasingly, over these years, we'll point the way. Yet, you'll have to choose your direction. Don't let this realization scare you. You'll love these upcoming years and the freedom which accompanies them.

Just remember what Uncle Ben said in *Spiderman*: "With great power comes great responsibility."

As you become older and have more power to make your decisions, you have the responsibility to make good ones. That's the purpose of this book, to offer some advice about how to navigate these next few years in your life.

The chapters in this book consist of two different voices. One is my mine. I've been where you are. I vividly remember what it's like to be your age. Because of this, I recognize certain paths serve you well to avoid while others should be embraced. I hope my experiences—positive and negative—help you see the difference.

There's another voice within these pages—a voice greater than mine. It's God's voice, revealed through scripture. Just like your parents, God wants what's best for us which is why He gave us rules and principles to follow. Everything in His Word is written to protect and provide for us. If we follow Him, He'll bless our paths.

I hope you enjoy this book. As you read, please write down your questions and observations, and find a trustworthy adult with whom you can discuss them. With the guidance of wisdom and discernment, your next seven years will be even better than your first twelve.

POPULARITY

WHEN I WAS IN SIXTH grade, I developed my very first crush on a girl: Sherry. I suppose I should clarify Sherry was the first girl I had a crush on whom I actually knew. I had a small thing for Julie on *The Love Boat*, but my admiration was pretty short-lived. Sherry was the first girl I ever really liked who actually looked at me and talked to me . . . and when she did, my heart turned flips!

My love for Sherry lasted throughout my sixth grade year, but even though I had reason to believe she liked me also, nothing ever came of it. Why? I was absolutely terrified to tell her how I felt. We sometimes walked together or passed a silly note, but that was it. I was too chicken to say anything about my feelings.

There's another reason why my sixth grade love went unfulfilled. As the year went on, Sherry began to change. She was a very pretty girl, at least I thought so, but she seemed to get prettier every month. By the end of the year, she turned the head of every middle school boy in the school!

You might think the situation was a good thing for Sherry . . . and for me as her admirer. The truth is, as she blossomed, things changed between us. Sherry rose in the social ranks of Tyro Junior High School rather quickly and became the most popular girl in our grade. I was just average, old Matthew known by friends, but mostly ignored by the popular crowd.

Alas, adolescent love can't flourish under such conditions. In fact, even friendships between different social groups can be strained. By the time we were in the eighth grade, Sherry and I hardly ever talked, anymore. By the time we were in high school, we barely even acknowledged one another.

IS POPULARITY A WORTHWHILE GOAL?

At this point, you might be tempted to feel sorry for me. After all, I obviously wasn't popular in school. Looking back, though, I actually feel sorrier for Sherry than for me. The pressure she faced to be pretty and funny enough, and, well, whatever enough to stay at the top of the social ladder was intense.

I'll tell a little more about her story later in this chapter. For now just know the pressure took its toll on her. It changed her life in a negative way. Many of you can probably relate because Sherry's tragic story isn't unique.

For kids in middle school, popularity seems like an important goal. Fueled by television shows, movies, books, and magazines, millions of teens feel pressured to dress the right way and talk the right way, and do the right things to make the right people approve. Most kids firmly believe without the approval of the *in crowd* they're nobody, so they willingly sacrifice anything necessary to win such approval.

It's a shame so many kids swallow this lie . . . and it *is* a lie. Sure, on the surface it feels great to win the approval of the crowd, but at what cost? The price tag for popularity is steep. It often requires more than anyone expects.

Let me ask you: What does it take to win the acceptance of your peers, to get a thumbs-up or stamp of approval from the crowd? Is there some sort of mental checklist to which your peers refer?

Do they look at other kids and say: Wardrobe? Check . . . that measures up. Hairstyle? Yeah, that'll do. Does he or she talk about the right things? Does he or she play the right sports? Does he or she have the right friends, watch the right television shows, and attend the right parties?

Who decides which criterion belongs on the list?

More importantly, if everyone in your school is being judged by such a checklist, and everyone is trying to fit in, how does anyone learn to think independently? How does anyone become his or her authentic self?

In other words, if everyone tries to conform to the list, then everyone tries to dress, talk, and act exactly alike. Meaning, nobody really gets to be unique. Nobody gets to be comfortable. Instead, everyone constantly tries to be something they're not. Why? They want other people to somehow say, "I accept you because you're just like me."

DEFINING YOU

I don't know about you, but I don't like the sound of that. I wouldn't want to live in a world where everyone acted, dressed, and sounded exactly alike any more than I want to live in a world where houses were the same style or flowers were the same color. God designed variety in His creation, including you and me!

Besides, when we allow someone else to tell us who we should or shouldn't be we give the person a power which only belongs to God. He created and made us uniquely. He gave each of us a one-of-a-kind set of fingerprints and an original personality. He also gave each of us a set of individual tastes, preferences, and abilities. These things make us who we are.

How tragic when we abandoned the unique characteristics God has given us so we can look and act like everyone else. In Romans 12:2, the Bible reads: *"Do not conform any longer to the pattern of this world, but be transformed by the renewing of your mind."*

Notice two things about this scripture. First, Paul warns us not to conform to the pattern of this world. To conform means to become like or to be similar to. So, Paul urges us not to be like the rest of the world. He says, "Don't follow their pattern. Break the mold!" Why? Well, I've already mentioned God uniquely made us, but there's another reason.

You see, the pattern of this world doesn't honor God. If you don't believe me, spend a few minutes tonight watching the evening news. The people of this world are violent and angry. They lie, cheat, and steal. They do all kinds of things which displease God.

So, to conform to the patterns of the world means to embrace their type of lifestyle. It means to go along with the crowd even when we don't like where they are going. Many things people do to fit in—conform—are things they know are wrong, but they do them hoping to be accepted.

Paul tells us to break the pattern. He basically says, "Hey, don't be like everyone else. Be transformed by God instead." The word transformed means to be changed. In essence, Paul says, "Instead of being just like everyone else so they'll accept you, let God change you to be more like Him. His opinion is the only one that really matters. Let God shape you into His image."

Here's the thing: if we do what Paul suggests, and we try to please God instead of everyone else, we'll ultimately have something most people long for—genuine peace.

THE ALTERNATIVE

I promised to tell you the rest of Sherry's story. Each year she became more beautiful, more popular. She had a great smile and sense of humor. God gave her so many gifts.

However, Sherry wasted them, or, at least, damaged them. She was so intent on fitting in with her popular friends she started doing whatever they told her to do. Even when she knew her actions were wrong.

She experimented with alcohol and sex. She dumped her old friends to make new ones who were bad influences in every way. By the time she reached high school, she had stopped caring about school for the most part. Her mind was elsewhere.

When Sherry was in the tenth grade, she became pregnant and dropped out of school altogether. That's the last I heard about her. I don't know if she graduated from high school. I don't know if she ever pulled her life together—I certainly hope she did! I only know her pursuit of popularity changed the trajectory of her entire life.

I pray for Sherry sometimes, and hope so much she found Jesus. Lots of people have turned to Him after they have made big mistakes. He's definitely able to put their lives back together, but there's also an extra blessing when a person's life doesn't crash.

That's why I encourage you to not trade the good thing God has given you for the temporary approval of your friends. Their approval will eventually come to an expected end and you'll be left to pick up the pieces alone. I know because I've been there. I've made mistakes which still haunt me.

A BAD TRADE

When I was in seventh grade one of my best friends was a kid named Todd who lived near me. Todd and I used to get together and play—he was one of the first kids I knew who had a real computer, and we played games on it after school nearly every day.

I liked Todd. He was nice, but he had a flaw: he wasn't popular at all. In fact, he was sort of awkward—the type of kid other kids made fun of.

I wasn't like that. I know I previously wrote I wasn't popular, but I wasn't unpopular either. I was just an average kid, and I wanted to be accepted. I started to worry my friendship with Todd might hurt my reputation.

What if hanging out with Todd made others look at me differently? What if the kids who picked on Todd started to pick on me, too?

My mind raced with the possibilities.

I was so worried I knew I had to act. Here's what I did: I dumped Todd as a friend. I ignored him at school and stopped going to his house in the afternoons. I didn't even give him an explanation.

For four years we had been buddies. Then, one day I just stopped talking to him. I felt awful about it, but I did it, anyway. I chose the approval of people I didn't know over the friendship I had already formed. I'm sad to admit I've barely spoken to Todd since.

You're probably shocked right now. Maybe you're even disappointed in me. You know what? You should be. I'm disappointed in myself. I can tell you this, if I could go back in time and change the way I acted, I'd do it.

Obviously I can't. I have to live with my mistake. I just hope by sharing my inexcusable behavior with you, you'll avoid making a similar mistake.

So, here's my advice: Don't ever allow anyone else to define you. Don't allow others to push you into doing something you know is wrong. Don't trade your conscience for their approval. It's simply not worth it.

By the way, time and maturity has taught me a secret about popularity which I didn't know at the time. If you don't try too hard to make people like you, and instead just relax and confidently be you, the kind of popularity you want will find you. People who really matter will like you . . . and you'll like you!

DEVOTION: Read Luke 15:11–32. As you read, think about where the son went wrong, and notice God's incredible grace to, once more, accept him.

CHAPTER

— *2* —

INSECURITY

To avoid criticism say nothing, do nothing, and be nothing.
—Aristotle (384–322 B.C.E.)

I ONCE SAW A CARTOON of a middle school student sitting at a table in the cafeteria. She sat hunched over her lunch. Over her head, the thought-bubble read: I CAN'T BELIEVE I WORE THIS OUTFIT TODAY. I BET EVERYONE IN THIS ROOM IS LAUGHING AT ME.

The second panel backed out to show the entire cafeteria, full of fellow students. Every one's thoughts were the same: I BET EVERYONE IS LAUGHING AT ME.

Ah, middle school, the land of the awkward and home of the insecure. There's something about the age group which promotes perfect paranoia—perfect, utter paranoia.

Try to say that without spitting!

No kidding. The idea everyone watches and judges your every thought, word, or action is a hallmark of teen years. It often leads to dark places.

Let me tell you a story about someone who experienced this. I could give you tons of examples from my observations of other people, but here's one person who hits a little closer to home: me.

Middle school insecurity created some real problems for me because of Sherry, the girl I mentioned in the last chapter. She and some other friends really gave me a taste of my own medicine.

RISE AND FALL OF A TEENAGE LEGEND

I told you in the last chapter I didn't exactly run with the popular crowd when I was a teenager. This was true . . . nearly. I did have a brief season when I tried to be really cool.

I always had a great sense of humor, and during my eighth grade year I started to use it for evil! Okay, that's not true, but I did enjoy making kids laugh. Since kids seemed to like me better when I was cracking jokes, I kept up a constant barrage of smart comments. Even at inappropriate times, or about inappropriate subjects.

I was always ready with some little blurb guaranteed to lighten the mood . . . and people responded. As a result, when my final year of middle school opened I made new friends, and I felt my popularity grow.

Before I go forward with this fascinating trip down memory lane, I need to clarify my rise in popularity came at a price. I've already told you how I abandoned an old friend. My new friends were bound by peer scrutiny and were very image-conscious. In other words, they were people who always had to wear the right clothes, say the right things, and look cool at all times. I definitely felt pressure to do the same.

I wanted to fit in, and when I was around them I felt like the kid in the cartoon I described earlier. It seemed everyone's eyes rested on me. They waited for me to mess up, and I did . . . well, sort of.

In October/November, my English teacher gave a test I had studied for; I knew the answers. At the time, I sat at a table with three other friends. On my left sat Sherry, of who I was no longer enamored; on her other side sat Justin, a good friend.

Sherry had not studied for the test, and when the teacher wasn't looking she whispered for me to move my arm so she could copy my answers. Instantly, I knew I had to make a decision. If I let her copy my paper, she'd be happy with me. I wanted her approval, but I did not want to cheat.

Cheating is wrong, and if we had been caught, the act might have resulted in each of us receiving a zero on the test. I wasn't okay with that. Sherry might not have cared if she received a zero, but I did. It just wasn't worth it.

So, in that instant, I made up my mind. I shook my head no and I continued taking my test. I still remember Sherry's shocked expression. Apparently, people didn't say no to her very often.

Sherry eyed me for a second, and then her expression turned from surprise to anger. She whispered something to the people around her, and their expressions became angry, too. That's the moment when everything changed.

That afternoon, Justin, sat in a different seat on the bus. When I tried to sit with him the next morning, he suggested I find somewhere different to be seated. Sherry stopped speaking with me altogether, and her other friends followed suit. Just that quickly, I felt like the entire world had turned against me, and I didn't have a funny comment to change things.

I went home that day feeling sad, confused, and devastated. I woke up feeling the same way. When I went to school again, I remember looking around and feeling certain everyone was watching me. What's more, I was sure they didn't like what they saw.

THE POWER OF NEGATIVE THINKING

Unfortunately, my story had a dark ending . . . at least, during the remainder of my eighth grade year. Somehow, I convinced myself because of my offense against Sherry, no one liked me, anymore—I felt sure of it. I walked around and watched everyone watch me. I tried to guess what they were thinking.

The backlash I experienced from the cheating disaster was really a dark season in my life. I still had friends at school and in church, but I didn't trust them. While I sat in class, walked the hallway, or rode the bus, I felt awkward, heavy, and lonely.

I stopped telling jokes, and didn't laugh or smile much. My social life crumbled, and my grades suffered. I felt I had stepped into a sort of pit. My confidence had been shot to pieces, and the insecurity that replaced it affected almost everything.

It's funny how as I write these words twenty-four years later, the whole debacle seems so silly. Taking a look back through adult lenses, I'm able to see things I wasn't able to recognize when I was fourteen years old.

I wish I could go back, talk to eighth grade me, and tell him how to handle the situation. Since I can't do that, I'm taking advantage of the next best thing. I'll share some things with you to, hopefully, help you avoid falling into a similar trap. The following are some lessons I learned from my experience with middle school insecurity:

LESSON NO. 1:

Very few people care what the Sherrys and friends of the world think of you. Let's start there.

A few classmates blew my world apart because I let them. I believed they had some strange power over people because they were pretty and popular. I believed everyone wanted to follow their lead, but that was not true.

Since I've become older, I see the entire scene differently. Yes, many kids opted to follow the lead of certain kids in our class. They attempted to dress and talk like them. Certainly, many kids in my eighth grade class wanted to be friends with them. In reality, though, they weren't.

Sherry didn't have a wide circle of friends because her inner circle didn't accept most other kids. This meant most kids didn't really know them well. Yet, most kids knew me.

Up until the time I drew my line in the cheating sand, I had tried to be warm and friendly to kids in my classes—most kids liked me. If I had just remembered my good standing with the majority of my classmates, and held true to the friendships I had already established, those kids would've stood by me. Well, at least, most of them. I didn't give them enough credit.

I assumed my friends didn't like me, anymore. So, I pulled away from them. As a result, they stepped back from me, too. I blamed Sherry, but it was actually my fault. Sherry didn't mess up most of those relationships. I did when I refused to trust my friends.

LESSON NO. 2:

People judge us by how we present ourselves to and treat them. This point goes along with the last one, but I want to expand it: whether we are teenagers or adults, other people make judgments about us based on what we let them see. If we let them see the good inside of us, they'll positively respond. In fact, they want to respond to our good nature. People are hungry for kindness.

You probably think it's more complicated than this, but it's really not. Why? Well, because other people are insecure, too. While we're wondering if they like us, they're wondering if we like them.

If we show people we do like them by treating them well, laughing at their jokes, and including them in our conversations, they'll usually reciprocate. At the very least, they'll walk away thinking, *Wow, what a great guy! I really like him!*

However, if we shut people out, or ignore them, others really can't get to know us. The only thing they can say is, "Well, I don't really know him. He doesn't seem very nice."

Here's my point: people are pretty simple. There's nothing mysterious about making friends. Be brave enough to show people who you are. As long as you're kind and warm, they'll respond favorably to you!

LESSON NO. 3:

Don't allow others to define your worth. You don't need the approval of other people to feel good about you. I know this might sound like a very parental thing to say, but it isn't any less true. On the contrary, there's a great, important truth in the statement.

Don't give other people the power to define or place value on you. Don't allow them to decide who you should or shouldn't be, and then hold you to the standard. If you let people label you, you'll fall into the trap of always trying to please them.

The need to please is a lot like shooting at a moving target. As soon as you please one group of people, there'll be another group wanting something different!

By the way, this doesn't mean you should ignore the advice of other people. It certainly doesn't mean you should neglect self-improvement.

On the contrary, living as a Christian means constantly evaluating ourselves based on scripture. We should admit where we fall short, and strive to grow and improve. We do this for the approval of the only One who matters, Jesus. Amen!

Even then, however, we must understand as long as we're in our bodies, on this planet, we can never reach His standard of perfection. So, we strive to be the best people we can be, accept His grace, and then relax in Him.

LESSON NO.4:

Every kid in school is as insecure as you are. As much as anything, I want you to know this fact. The cartoon I mentioned earlier was exactly right. If you were able to read the thoughts of everyone else at your school—which might, admittedly, be frightening and disturbing—you'd find everyone feels as insecure as you do, everyone.

In fact, try to picture the one person in your school who's so cool you're absolutely certain he or she never feels insecure. Have you captured the image of the person? Good.

Let me clue you in on something. The person you envision is just as insecure as you. Perhaps, maybe even more.

○   Lots of times, people mask insecurity behind wisecracks, cool clothes, boasting, and strutting. They pretend they have it all together, but it's more than likely just a show.

Do you remember what we talked about in chapter 1? Middle school popularity often comes with a price. So often, kids feel pressured by peers to say the right things, wear the right clothes, and react to every situation in just the right way. If they don't, they feel less worthy, important, and liked.

Seriously, this effort has got to be exhausting! Not to mention, it's also unnecessary. Relax in the knowledge your classmates aren't experts whose opinions you must follow. Instead, just like you, they're unsure and insecure, trying to learn who they are also.

So, what does all this mean?

No one in middle or high school has it all together. You can come close if you remember this fact: you're fearfully and wonderfully made, as stated in Psalm 139—one of my favorite scriptures.

The psalmist reminds us God created us inside of our mothers' wombs. He actually says God "knitted us together"—*what a cool image*—and on that day He knew all about us, He loved us. Before we had ever accomplished one thing, said a single word, or made an appearance in the world, God loved us. He loves us because He made us. That's enough for Him!

Keep this in mind. Repeat it every day. God made you in His image, and He loves you right now. Knowing this changes everything. Think about it—because of God's love:

- You don't need to try so hard to impress people.
- You can stop worrying about whether or not you're worthy of admiration.

- You can take a breath and say, "I was made in the image of God, and He has plans for me; I matter!"
- You can freely be you.

Let's return to the scene described in the aforesaid cartoon. Imagine you're sitting in the cafeteria. All around you are kids who keep one eye on their plate and one eye on the rest of the room. Everyone is thinking the same thing: *I bet everyone is watching me.*

Now, imagine in the middle of the room one kid is different. This kid isn't watching anyone else. He isn't worried about who may be watching him. Instead, he eats his lunch in peace, talks to his friends, and laughs and enjoys himself.

He really is different from the other kids, but in a good way. He isn't worried about whether or not people like what he's wearing, how he combs his hair, or when he talks in the hall if he uses the cool new catch-phrase.

This kid seems oblivious to such worries. He simply eats, talks, and smiles. He seems happy, confident, and peaceful.

You can be that kid, you really can! Just take a breath, relax, and thank God you're fearfully and wonderfully made.

DEVOTIONS: Read Psalm 139. What do you learn about God in this passage? What do you learn about you?

CHAPTER

— 3 —

SEX

I WAS IN THE THIRD grade when my dad and I had "the talk." I remember it well. I had heard some kids talking about sex at school. As I remember, they had used an inappropriate word, and I wanted to know what they were talking about. So, I asked my mother. She, in turn, sent me straight to my father.

As usual, he was at his workshop tinkering with some project. I sidled up close to him and cleared my throat.

I said, "Dad, can I ask you a question?"

Without looking up he said, "Okay."

When I asked my question: he froze. One minute later, I sat on a stool beside his workbench as he explained the birds and the bees. I must confess I didn't understand a single word he said!

Maybe you've had a similar experience. After all, the first time you hear about sex it makes absolutely no sense! I mean, can you be expected to grasp the concept of sex when you're grossed out by the thought of holding hands?

This is why I'm including this chapter—I want a chance to re-mind you of some important things you need to know. Why so important? Because over the next few years, you're going to hear kids talk about sex, a lot. Unfortunately, 99 percent of what they're going to say is untrue!

A DANGEROUS MESSAGE

If you really pay attention to the things other kids say about sex in middle school, you're going to be confused. Most of what's being said doesn't even make sense. Kids are simply repeating things they've heard, or seen in some movie or, maybe, just imagined.

The truth is, very few kids in middle school really know a whole lot about sex. Everyone wants to act like an expert, but very few fully understand what they're saying.

This may not seem like a big deal, but it actually matters. Those sexual jokes, references, and boasts communicate three big lies about sex—each one unhealthy and dangerous. Let's examine each one:

The first lie kids communicate: everyone is doing it. Even in middle school, everyone wants to act like they have had a sexual encounter. They claim this because it's considered cool, and lots of kids feel ashamed to admit they're sexually pure. Everyone pretends they're doing things, and everyone assumes everyone else is doing things, too.

So, let me start by setting your mind at ease. Everyone isn't doing it, not in middle school. Not even in high school. In fact, a recent poll[1] suggests nearly 70 percent of students entering college are virgins. This number saddens me because it should be higher. Yet, the percentage also reassures me—it suggests well over half of graduating high school seniors, in fact, remain sexually pure.

---

1   Michael Foust, "70% of High School Students Are Virgins, Study Reports," by Baptist Press, October 15, 2010, http://www.bpnews.net/bpnews.asp?ID=33877 (accessed August 20, 2012)

In middle school, the number of students who remain sexually pure is much higher. So, no, everyone isn't doing it.

Even more disturbing is a second big lie: everyone should be doing it. If you listen to the things other kids say, you'd assume normal teenage behavior includes sex. Movies and television shows certainly echo this message: sex for teenagers is normal, healthy, and right as long as they love one another.

Funny how movies and television shows love to depict how wonderful sex can be for unmarried teens, but they usually neglect to tell the entire story. We rarely see a teen at the doctor's office after contracting some horrible, incurable sexually transmitted disease (STD); with a baby he or she isn't ready to care for; or with a broken sense of what being loved really means.

Sex isn't the game these movies or some kids pretend it is. It's a wonderful gift from God intended to be experienced in marriage.

GOD'S DESIGN

Before I mention the third lie about sex, let me reiterate what I just wrote: God created sex. It isn't bad, dirty, wrong, or dangerous as long as it's used as God intended. God created sex, but He placed it within certain boundaries reserved for husbands and wives, inside the marriage union. In that context, sex is beautiful and pure.

So, why does God restrict it? Why doesn't He allow people to have sex with anyone at any time they desire? Some reasons go beyond my capacity to explain, but I'll focus on the obvious. God restricts sex to marriage because He cares for us, and wants what's best for us; sex is too important and powerful to be treated casually.

If this is confusing, you need to understand **the third big lie about sex is: it's just sex**. In other words, lots of people perceive sex as a physical action and nothing more; like eating or exercising. In their view, sex means nothing beyond a moment of pleasure. However, this perception shows a great misunderstanding of God's design.

You see, anytime two people engage in sexual activity, more happens than just a random joining of bodies. Even though the two involved often don't realize this, the Bible teaches sex goes beyond the physical. Something spiritual, emotional, and powerful occurs when a couple shares this gift God has given them. In addition to joining bodies, they join their spirits and emotions—the two become one.

Now, stay with me for a moment. In marriage, what I just described is a good thing. It strengthens the bond between a husband and wife. They are safe, wholly committed to one another, and secure in the knowledge each will solely give himself or herself to the other for the rest of their lives.

Armed with this knowledge, as the years go by, the husband and wife continue to grow closer to one another. Sex is part of their increased closeness. This is God's design.

Yet, everything is different with unwed sexual partners. They haven't pledged commitment to one another. They haven't vowed before God to keep themselves only for one another forever. So, eventually, when the newness of their relationship wears thin, and they break up, the part of their hearts and souls which were once joined during sexual encounters is ripped apart.

This separation causes deep and tremendous emotional and mental anguish. Remember, the two had become one through sex. Yet, when their tie is severed they, once more, are two separate entities. The hurt experienced goes beyond broken-heartedness. Each person has lost part of his or her sense of self which can't be recovered (apart from God's grace).

Now, combine the scenario described with the risk of STDs and pregnancy, and it's plain to see why God reserved the gift of sex for the marriage relationship. There's no such thing as just sex. Sex is meaningful and powerful, and it shouldn't ever be used haphazardly.

SO, WHAT DOES THIS MEAN FOR YOU?

While you are still young, you need to embrace the truth. The enemy has blinded our culture, including many of your friends, with lies about sex. These lies bring with them pain and dysfunction. God, on the other hand, loves you. He only wants to protect and provide for your future. So, look to Him, embrace His way, and you'll find you can avoid the pain associated with sexual promiscuity.

However, if you've already become sexually active, it's not too late to start over. Speak with your pastor, youth pastor, or another Christian adult you trust about God's healing and how to recommit to purity.

Remember, everyone's not doing it. Everyone shouldn't be doing it. It isn't meaningless or unimportant. Sex is wonderful, powerful, meaningful, and reserved. Wait for God's timing, wait for marriage. I promise you won't regret waiting!

GUARDING OUR EYES

Having discussed sexual activity let me point out one more sexual snare which, in some ways, is even more prevalent. It has to do with your eyes and the images they absorb every day in our culture.

From movies to television shows to video games to billboards, we are surrounded by cultural icons and images, and nearly every one of them sends a disturbing message about sex.

Think about how women and men seen in these mediums are usually dressed, but don't think about it too long! They usually wear revealing clothing which is tight and short. The idea is to seem sexually appealing, and it works. Men and women, alike, fix their gaze on these images and struggle to turn away.

Unfortunately, these images do more than sell products. They affect us in a deep way. The pictures enter through our eyes, and go straight to our minds. As a result, our minds start to produce some unhealthy thoughts which are sexual in nature.

The technical term for these thoughts and their associated feelings is lust. According to Jesus, lust is a problem, a big problem. In fact, in Matthew 5 He said when we look at another person and think lustful thoughts, we have committed a sin.

Harsh, isn't it? After all, we're all guilty of thinking unhealthy thoughts sometimes. God's standard is high which is why we all need His grace. However, don't lose sight of one thing: God wants what's best for us. When we allow our minds to dwell on sinful things, He knows the direction such thoughts will take us. That's why Jesus tells us to be so careful to guard our minds.

I can almost hear your next question: how do I control what I'm thinking? Well, I'm glad you asked!

PORTALS TO OUR MINDS

The doorway to our minds is through our eyes and ears. What I mean is the things we see and hear feed our minds. It's like eating. Healthy food nourishes the body while a steady diet of junk food can make us ill. Likewise, reading, watching, and listening to godly things leads our thinking in a healthy direction. Visual junk food can make us sick.

Let's bring this around to the topic at hand. I mentioned pop-culture has a terrible message regarding sex. Nearly every medium sends a message indicating sex is a game, and women are just beautiful objects used for enjoyment.

These mediums fill our eyes with the worst kind of visual junk food. They capture pictures of women in all sorts of poses and skimpy outfits. Sometimes, they project pictures of women in no outfits at all. There's a term for these types of pictures: pornography.

There are so many things to stress about this topic—more than I can possibly cover in this book. For now, I'll focus on three main truths I want you to know about pornography.

1. **Pornography is deceptive**. The pornographic pictures in magazines or on billboards aren't real. They show altered images of models enhanced by lights and computers so they look über-attractive, more attractive than real people look. Maybe you don't think it's a big deal, but you would be wrong. See, people who spend time looking at pornography become so enamored with altered images they lose the ability to appreciate real people. Suddenly, real people, whose bodies haven't been altered by computers—and who actually have thoughts and emotions—aren't good enough. Lots of times, regular viewers of these images have trou-

ble developing and maintaining healthy relationships. They wind up alone and lonely. How sad is that?

2. **Pornography is addictive**. Maybe when you were in the fifth grade, a Drug Abuse Resistance Education (D.A.R.E.) officer talked with your class about addictive drugs. Well, believe it or not, pornography is an addiction, too. Viewing such images excites certain chemicals in the brain. Once this happens, the brain wants more. Even though it's so unhealthy, even though viewing it ruins relationships, and even though it inspires lustful thoughts the brain wants more. Some people who get hooked on pornography have to spend months in support groups to get help to break their addiction.

3. **Pornography can lead viewers to bad places**. People who view pornography always get more than they bargained for, and not in a good way! It's similar to drinking salt water—it doesn't quench the thirst, and leaves viewers wanting more! Pornographic images messes up thinking so much, viewers lose their sense of right and wrong. They start to act in ways they never would've acted before. For instance, people who view pornography start to think of sex as a sport. Instead of appreciating it as God's gift, they see it as a conquest: *with how many people can I have sex?* We've already talked about the dangers of a pornography-addicted lifestyle which can even go further. If the cycle doesn't stop, the mind can become so polluted viewers commit crimes against the objects of their

desires, and can't see the harm in doing so! Pornography viewing can lead to dark places.

Just to be clear, I'm not suggesting pornographic viewing will turn you into a criminal! I'm warning it's not worth it. Pornography isn't healthy in any way. It destroys healthy thinking about sex, and leads to places you don't want to go.

That's why you need to be so careful about what you allow into your eye gate. You can't ignore every image, I get that. To avoid them altogether, you'd have to walk around with your eyes closed which is seemingly a recipe for disaster!

I just want you to be wise. When your friends want to watch a movie you know is filled with inappropriate imagery, find something else to do. When they're staring at a magazine your conscience tells you is unsuitable, don't join them. Guard your eye gate, and in the process, you'll guard your mind and heart as well.

SO, WHAT DOES ALL THIS MEAN?

Bottom line: sex is a gift from God. It's not bad, dirty, or sinful. God created it, and that alone means its original intent is good! You don't have to blush or giggle mischievously when you hear the word—sex is a part of life, married life.

The problem with this world: whenever God gives a good gift, humans eventually twist it into something bad. Think about it, anything that's good can also be corrupted. A fire burning in the fireplace is good. A fire burning curtains is a problem! Words used in love or appreciation are good. Words used to demean or cut down are bad.

Sex is no different—in marriage, sex is a wonderful gift. Outside of marriage sex causes many problems and damages many lives. We need to use God's gift in the way He asks us to use it!

Over the next few years, you'll see more people ignore this principle than anything else in this book. Our culture doesn't like God's rules about sex. People say His rules are old-fashioned, ancient, and outdated. According to popular opinion, people today are smarter and more sophisticated. They're enlightened.

Ask yourself: Do people today know more than God? Have people really become so brilliant they know things God doesn't know?—of course, not.

God's plan is just as real today as it ever was. He doesn't force it on you. If you choose to follow Him, even though it may mean making some sacrifices right now, you'll grow up in a healthy way which will allow you to enter marriage one day with your heart in tact. If you don't follow Him, there will be consequences, even though you may not see them for quite some time.

That's why I want to end this chapter by asking you to imagine you ten, fifteen, or maybe twenty years from now. Try to imagine the grown up you getting ready for your wedding. I wonder what Future You wants to say to Teenage You at that moment.

Future You will probably say, "Don't forget to exercise. I need to keep my figure!" Or, "Make sure you pay attention in math class. You really will use this stuff someday!"

I'll bet anything Future You will say, "Thank you so much for deciding now to handle sex God's way. I know it's tough—I remember how impossible it seemed. Today, however, I wouldn't trade that decision for anything. I'm getting married today, and it sure feels good to enter marriage knowing we've saved ourselves for each other, just like God intended. Our marriage is already off to a good start. So, thank you!

Oh, and don't forget to floss!"

DEVOTIONS: Read 1 Corinthians 6:18–20. What makes sexual sin different from others? Why does God have the right to speak to this area of your life?

CHAPTER

— 4 —

WORRY, STRESS, AND THE PURSUIT OF PERFECTION

LET'S PLAY A GAME! I'M going to describe a situation, and then you describe the outcome.

Imagine a water-pipe with a major blockage. The blockage is possibly hair, grease . . . a Nerf basketball—it's your choice. It's really not important to the crux of the story.

Now, imagine the pipe is under incredible pressure. On one end, a wall of water is pushing against the blockage. On the other, the blockage holds fast. Increasingly more water flows in, and pushes against the wall. Yet, the wall can't move—it's stuck.

Now, here's the question: what'll happen to the pipe?

If you're having trouble with an answer, try a different scenario. Imagine you're filling a balloon with water. However, you don't stop as it starts to become full. You feel the sides tighten, but you keep filling it.

You hear the latex start to stretch, but you keep filling it. You feel the tension of the balloon, knowing it can't hold one more ounce, yet you refuse to stop.

Same question: what will happen to the balloon?

The answer is the same in both scenarios: explosion! The pipe and balloon will eventually give way to the incredible pressure inside and burst open, causing who knows what kind of damage—you'll be forced to spend time mopping the floor or drying the carpet. That's a result of the incredible power of pressure.

Pressure is the force of one object against another object. When harnessed for good, scientists and engineers can use the force of pressure in incredible ways. When they fail to control it, however, an explosion occurs and results in a big mess, and maybe even pain.

You might see where I'm going with this. In our lives, the pressure of worry and stress works much the same way.

We all have different daily pressures in life—time, work, and performance. In your life, these pressures present themselves in the form of: preparing for school every morning, finishing work in a timely manner, studying and performing well on tests and quizzes, practicing to improve playing the guitar, fulfilling household responsibilities, and more. Each goal places a certain amount of pressure on our lives.

When we manage daily pressures the correct way, they're actually good for us. They keep us sharp, and push us to do our best. However, when we don't keep the pressures of our lives under control, we eventually experience the same phenomenon as an overfilled water balloon: some type of an explosion!

I should know. It happened to me.

MY EXPLOSION

When I turned thirteen years old, my life looked pretty much like everybody else's I knew. I worked reasonably hard in school and made good grades. I played basketball in two different community leagues. I marched in the school band, took piano lessons, and stayed active in my Boy Scout Troop, and my church youth group. In other words, I was a normal, busy thirteen-year-old kid.

Unfortunately, on top of all my activities, I had one additional hobby: I worried . . . about everything. Though I never really told anyone about it, I spent a great deal of time thinking through the details of my life and worrying about random possibilities. Maybe you have done this, too.

I worried about my friends at school. *What if they stopped liking me?* I worried about my family. *What if something happens to one of my parents?* I worried about succeeding in school or at one of my activities. *What if I'm not good enough?* I worried about my future. *What if I don't achieve my dreams?*

The truth is I worried about anything there was to be worried about. In fact, when I heard a teacher say worrying was unhealthy and potentially harmful to our bodies, I worried about that, too.

What was I doing to myself?

Looking back, I laugh at what a mess I became. Yet, at the time it was no laughing matter. All my worrying actually made me sick. I developed headaches which were so bad my parents kept me out of school.

In the beginning I missed a day or two, here or there. Later, I missed several days at a time. I didn't get over the headaches, and my troubles had just started; in the upcoming months things went from bad to worse.

Unsure why I felt so bad, so often, my parents eventually took me to the doctor. The doctor couldn't find a problem, so he sent me to a different doctor. The second doctor eventually sent me to another location where the doctors ran tests and considered possibilities.

I had my eyes and teeth checked, blood drawn, and brain scanned. No one was able to diagnose the cause of my illness. That is, until one day when a doctor sat me down and looked into my eyes.

He said, "I think I know what's happening. You need to learn how to handle worry and stress."

Right there in the doctor's office, I started to learn the fine art of letting go. To be honest, I never truly mastered it, but I did make significant improvements. My headaches disappeared and so did my long, drawn-out worry-parties.

I didn't get rid of all of the pressure inside of me. I did, however, learn to manage the pressure. It started with understanding an important passage from the Bible.

WHAT JESUS SAYS ABOUT WORRY

Take a moment to read the following passage which Jesus spoke during His "Sermon on the Mount" in Matthew 6:

> "Therefore I tell you, do not worry about your life, what you will eat or drink; or about your body, what you will wear. Is not life more than food, and the body more than clothes? [26] Look at the birds of the air; they do not sow or reap or store away in barns, and yet your heavenly Father feeds them. Are you not much more valuable than they? [27] Can any one of you by worrying add a single hour to your life?

[28] "And why do you worry about clothes? See how the flowers of the field grow. They do not labor or spin. [29] Yet I tell you that not even Solomon in all his splendor was dressed like one of these. [30] If that is how God clothes the grass of the field, which is here today and tomorrow is thrown into the fire, will he not much more clothe you—you of little faith? [31] So do not worry, saying, 'What shall we eat?' or 'What shall we drink?' or 'What shall we wear?' [32] For the pagans run after all these things, and your heavenly Father knows that you need them. [33] But seek first his kingdom and his righteousness, and all these things will be given to you as well. [34] Therefore do not worry about tomorrow, for tomorrow will worry about itself. Each day has enough trouble of its own.

Imagine how shocking these words were for people to hear. Jesus basically looked at them and said, "You need to stop worrying about your life and trust God to take care of you."

Do you know who He was addressing? His audience was mostly comprised of people struggling under Roman occupation. They lived in constant fear of what Roman soldiers may do to them. Many of them were poor, and the majority of them wondered where they'd get food to eat.

In other words, these people had problems, and now Jesus sat in front of them and instructed, "Don't worry?" How could He say such a thing?

The answer to this question is Jesus wanted people to understand an important truth: God is bigger than the details of our lives.

We may face big problems, but God dwarfs them. Even when they seem too big to handle, He can handle them.

Our challenge is learning to truly hand them over to God! In the following passage, Jesus teaches how to do this. He gives three categorical Rs to use to rise above worry and stress: refocus, release, and remember. Let's explore each step.

STEP 1: REFOCUS

Look again at the passage. Jesus tells people not to worry about clothes, food, or the details of life. Yet, those things seem like legitimate concerns. People have to eat, they need warm clothes. So, what does Jesus mean when He says to stop worrying about those important details of life?

To answer the question, re-read verse 33. Jesus says, *"But seek first His kingdom and His righteousness, and all these things will be given to you as well."* Allow me to translate this verse. We need to put God first, even above our needs. Focus on following and serving Him. Make that life's top priority. If we do, all of the other details of life—big and small—will fall into place.

That doesn't mean if we honor Jesus, life will be trouble-free! Certainly not! Jesus had plenty of trouble when He lived on this earth. Living for Him doesn't guarantee we'll always go to bed with a full stomach, be warm, do well financially, or that God will bless us with material possessions. Jesus didn't have those things when He lived on Earth, and we may not either.

On the contrary, Jesus knew as well as anyone life can be difficult which is actually His point in this passage. Life on Earth is filled with stress, turmoil, and uncertainty, but if we give these things the prime place in our thought-lives, they'll take control! They'll consume us so all we ever think about are the things that worry us, and all of our time is spent trying to deal with those things.

There's a better way. Focus on God and trust Him with the details of your life. You'll find His strength is sufficient for your greatest needs. He cares for you and is able to keep you. While He never promises to remove troubles from your life, He does promise to be with you as you go through them.

Turn to and trust Him. Even when life seems crazy, He can give you peace.

Refocus on God—the first step to overcome worrying and stress. We have to do this first, or we'll never be able to make the second step.

STEP 2: RELEASE

Think for a moment, and make a list of the things which tend to worry you the most. When you lie down in your bed at night, and those "what ifs" start to whisper into your ear, what do they say?

What if I flunk the test at school tomorrow? What if people don't like me? What if I get sick? What if my parents get a divorce? What if our house catches on fire?

I'm sure you can add plenty of what-ifs to the list.

Now, look at your list and think for another moment. How many things can you actually prevent? How many are under your control? How many are even influenced by you?

Okay, you have some control over the test, though your teacher has a big hand in it, too. You can't control what questions she asks, but you can study the material.

What about the other what ifs? You can't fully control if you get sick. You have no control over your parents' well-being. You can't fully protect your house from a fire. You can't completely control whether or not people like you.

Do you get the point? There are very few things in life which are completely, 100 percent under your control. Yet, most of us spend great amounts of time worrying about the very things we can't change!

Are hours spent worrying really accomplishing anything at all?

That's what Jesus meant in verse 27 when He said, *"Can any one of you by worrying add a single hour to your life?"*. He means worry doesn't help. It's not useful, healthy, or beneficial. That's why worry needs to be released. Simply let it go.

An American theologian named Reinhold Niebuhr once wrote: *"God grant me the serenity to accept the things I cannot change, the courage to change the things I can, and the wisdom to know the difference."*[2] This passage describes exactly what God calls us to do. He calls us to take care of the things we can take care of, and let the other things go. If we can't change or control them, we have to learn to give them to God.

So, how do we do this? When worry starts to creep in, and I feel my chest tighten and that old headache begins to rise, I have to do three things:

1. I stop and get still. Literally, I cease whatever I'm doing or thinking about and stand perfectly still.

2. I take a deep breath, hold it, and release it slowly. Sometimes I repeat this act two or three times to regain my composure.

---

2   Reinhold Niebuhr, *The Essential Reinhold Niebuhr: Selected Essays and Addresses*, ed. Robert McAfee Brown, (New Haven, CT: Yale University Press, 1987).

3. I pray: "Father, you know I'm worried and anxious right now. My eyes are in the wrong place, and I feel overwhelmed. Help me give this to you right now. I know you're big enough to handle it. Help me to let it go and trust you with it. Amen."

Now, here's the trick: after I pray this prayer I have to somewhat force myself to not think about it, anymore. Every time worries creep in, I have to say, "No. I won't worry. I gave that one to God."

We have to fight the battle in our minds. The mind is also critical to making the final step.

STEP 3: REMEMBER

The final step to overcoming worry in our lives involves memory. We need to pause and remember God's goodness and faithfulness. That is, how He has helped us in the past. If we can remember what He has done in the past, it'll help us trust Him more in the future.

Right now, try to remember one time during the past few years when you were really upset about something and took it to God in prayer. Can you remember a time? Now, think about how He answered your prayer.

When my wife, Tonya, and I got married, we weren't the richest folks in the world monetarily. Heck, we're still not! When our second baby was born—and Tonya decided to stop working to stay home with the kids—money was extra scarce. I wasn't making very much as a young teacher. Without her salary, we barely managed to pay the bills!

One month, things became especially bleak. Our daughter had been in the hospital with a really bad virus, and the doctor's bills were huge . . . and just kept coming! One day when I returned home from work, my wife was holding a bill in the amount of five hundred dollars. We had no money to pay it.

We really didn't know what to do, so we did the only thing we knew to do: we prayed. We asked God to somehow provide the money for us.

That night, I facilitated a Bible study for a small community group. After class, they presented me with a gift which they had collected the previous week before the bill had arrived in the mail.

When I opened the envelope, guess how much money I found inside: $501. God even gave us an extra dollar! That night, we got on our knees and thanked God like crazy for providing for us.

I shared this story to ask you this question: after that incident, do you think Tonya and I worry about money, anymore? The answer: only when we forget.

Every once in a while we lose sight of what happened in the past, and then find ourselves worried again. Every time we forget, we stop and remember the night when God gave us five hundred dollars, and then we relax.

God helped us in the past, so we can trust Him to help us in the future, too.

Whether or not you realize it, you also have this kind of story, many stories. You just need to stop and pay attention. When you release something to God, be sure to stand back and watch Him work.

Notice how He is able to keep you. Feel how much He loves you, and store them in your memory. Then later, when you feel worry creep back into your mind, replay those memories.

Remembering God's goodness and His past care gives us courage for the future. It renews our trust in Him. Those memories help us to refocus our eyesight from our problems onto Him which allows us to release our burdens and give them to God.

Later, after we've watched Him at work, we have brand new memories of His goodness to continue to strengthen our faith in Him. It's cyclical.

Concentrate on taking all three steps I've presented. Your worries will eventually decrease, and you'll experience peace.

PERFECTION'S PURSUIT

Before we finish this chapter, I want to mention one more thing. It has to do with a type of stress many of us create for ourselves by pursuing the wrong things.

Some people use all their time and energy in life chasing things which are bad for them, empty, or impossible to attain. The wrong pursuit is like aiming at the wrong target. You might hit it, but you're not going to hit an exact bull's-eye! That's why it's so important to stop and consider what you're really shooting for in life; set the right goals for you. Otherwise, you set yourself up for stress and frustration.

Imagine you have a history test in the morning, and you really want to get a good grade. You spend a significant amount of time studying and preparing. The next day you take this test, and feel good about it. However, when the teacher hands back the grades, you receive a B. Even though it seems like a good grade, you're unhappy.

I should've made an A, you think, *a B isn't good enough!*

The following week, on the night before the history test, you study again. This time, however, you care nothing about learning the material. You solely concentrate on getting an A. So, you spend the night trying to dump the material into your short-term memory.

This is hard, unsatisfying work. You feel tense and nervous—so much so you can't sleep well that night, and then you don't eat breakfast in the morning.

By the time you get to school you're exhausted and on-edge. When you get your test paper you make a slew of careless mistakes. The result: an even worse grade than the first time. Again, the next week when test time rolls around, the cycle is repeated, but the outcome is even worse.

Now, I ask you: What was your mistake? Was it trying to get an A? Certainly not!

There's nothing wrong with trying to earn an A on your test. There's nothing wrong with pushing yourself to do better. The problem surfaced when the need for a good grade overshadowed the real goal of the test—learning history. You pursued a grade instead of knowledge, and as a result of this wrong focus, worry and stress resulted.

Think how the story would be different if you said, "I'm going to learn this history assignment, and I hope to get an A on tomorrow's test." The next day you receive a B, and feel disappointed, but you think, *Wow, I should've done better, but, at least, I learned the material. Next week I'll try again; maybe I'll start to learn it earlier, ask more questions, or work slowly on my test. Whatever I do, I'll make sure I know my stuff next week . . . and then I'll try again.*

No matter what you make on the next test, you'll ultimately succeed. Why? You'll pursue the right goal which is learning history. You'll also save a great deal of unwanted worry and stress along the way.

There are two points to this scenario.

First, in life many people, who feel burdened by worry and stress, pursue the wrong things. They pursue promotions at work, bigger paychecks, fame, praise, power, or glory. Such goals bring no true joy or contentment. As a result, people who pursue them feel frustration and stress. After all, there's always a bigger paycheck, a bigger trophy, or a loftier record.

These things are great, but they aren't satisfying. The pursuit of them will never end. The result: constant stress, worry, and a nagging feeling of always falling short of the mark.

Your ultimate goals should be more satisfying things such as: knowledge, strength, growth, and relationships. Focus on improving as a person. Set goals which really matter, and let all of the other things take care of themselves—they will. The right pursuit helps you to relax and enjoy life more deeply.

Second, embrace a healthy dose of grace. No one is more frustrated than a failed perfectionist. In other words, remember each life consists of successes and failures.

During your life, you'll experience plenty of both. Learn to enjoy your successes and learn from your failures without allowing them to destroy your peace. Some of the greatest people in history fought through epic failures before they eventually succeeded.

Have you ever heard of Thomas Edison . . . Henry Ford . . . Albert Einstein? Each person failed repeatedly before he finally broke through.

Are these people too ancient for you? Well, what about Bill Gates, Walt Disney, or Steven Spielberg? If you Google their stories, you'll find these people stumbled often on their way to success. They gave themselves grace, however, and kept moving forward. That's because they weren't pursuing perfection. They pursued things that mattered so much more than that!

FINAL THOUGHT

I want to leave you with one final thought. My friend, David, who has gone through his fair share of trouble over the years, once told me his secret to avoid worry and stress.

He said, "Every time something happens to me, I always ask myself, 'will this really matter to me a year from now?' If the answer is no, then it's not worth worrying about today."

I think that's great advice. So, let me ask you: a year from today, what will really matter to you?

- That test you've been stressing over?
- The project that's due next month?
- That embarrassing incident on the playground?
- That chord you can't seem to hit on your guitar?
- That ugly shirt you had to wear to school last week?
- The wrong answer you gave in math class?
- That girl or boy who still doesn't like you?

What will really matter to you down the road? I have a hunch everything on this list will work itself out during the course of the next year. This is not to suggest you shouldn't study for the test, work hard on the project, practice the guitar, or think about your wardrobe. You should do all of those things.

Just remember to keep your focus in the correct target. Also, give yourself a healthy dose of grace when you fail. God has grace for you. Try to have some for you, too.

DEVOTIONS: Read Matthew 6 again. Ask God to help you learn to refocus, release, and remember.

CHAPTER

— 5 —

DECISION-MAKING

I WAS IN SIXTH GRADE the first time I heard the phrase "live for the moment." Well, maybe I heard it before that year, but until sixth grade, I never understood what these words meant. Then, I met Russell.

Russell transferred to my school during my sixth grade year, and we became instant friends. Truthfully, I'm not sure how we became friends. We were complete opposites.

I was a straight-laced, cautious, and obedient student. I was a little mischievous and quick with a laugh, but rarely got into trouble. On the other hand, Russell was loud, impetuous, and carefree. He was the kind of kid who put forth minimal effort on school assignments, but maximum effort on his many schemes . . . and there were many.

That's why, as I spent time with him that year, I became familiar with his favorite saying: "You've just got to live for the moment." Those words were usually followed by the suggestion of something crazy, reckless, dangerous, or even illegal. Russell seemingly never worried about the consequences; he always lived for the moment. The funny thing was the moment after Russell's schemes usually brought trouble.

I wonder sometimes what happened to Russell. Our friendship was short-lived. After sixth grade, we took different classes and I rarely found an opportunity to talk with him. From a distance, though, I watched him drift aimlessly through middle school. He was held back a few times, and then when he was sixteen he dropped out of school. That was the last I heard from Russell. In retrospect, living for the moment didn't seem to work so well for him.

A MOMENT CAN LINGER OR LAST

I was thinking about Russell, recently; particularly his desire to live for the moment as I read an article from the newspaper. It was the tragic story of two teenagers, Chris and Susan, and how one moment's bad decision led to another bad decision that turned into a tragedy. A moment in time that changed many lives for the worse.

The story started on a Friday night when the teens separately decided to attend a party in town. The party was unsupervised which meant there was no voice of reason in the house. Instead, the people who attended did whatever they wanted. Alcohol flowed freely, and the party quickly grew.

Sometime during the latter part of the night, or the earliest part of Saturday morning, a huge argument occurred. Susan left the party with several other teens, but she didn't stay away.

When her car pulled back into the driveway, Chris—who was still angry—spotted Susan and the teens with whom she had left, picked up a paving stone, and hurled it at the car's passenger side. The stone burst through the window and landed on Susan's lap.

He never thought it would lacerate her liver. Yet, it did. Within a few hours, Susan was dead. Just like that, the party ended in tragedy.

As I write, Susan's senseless death still affects so many people. Her friends and family obviously struggle to accept the fact she's gone. Chris does as well, but he struggles with his thoughts from a prison cell where he's serving time for her murder.

Of course, his friends and family miss him, too. By the time he gets out of jail, his entire youth will have disappeared. What a tragedy!

So many people are suffering. Why? A few bad decisions were made in a moment which lingered beyond the moment. Instead, they changed many lives forever.

THE LEGACY OF CHOICES

Before we go on, think about that story, and pick out the bad decisions these teenagers made:

- Attending the party was certainly a poor choice. At the very least, when they arrived and saw what was happening, they should've left, yet they chose to stay.

- Drinking alcohol was a bad decision. For one thing, the teens who drank alcohol were underage which meant their drinking was illegal. Of course, even if they had been of legal age, alcohol impairs judgment. People who drink too much do things they usually wouldn't do. Without the influence of alcohol, the entire night would've been different.

- Getting into a car after drinking alcohol was another poor decision. Everyone knows lives are at risk anytime they climb into a car with a drunk driver.

- Of course, Chris throwing the stone was a bad decision. He allowed his emotions to burn too hot, and he did something he'll regret every day for the rest of his life.

Now, look at the list again. Remove any one of these bad choices, this horrible story ends differently. The thing about actions, they never remain in the moment. They last—once we make them, we can't unmake them. We must live with our choices.

That's why it's so important to give careful thought to the things we do, even while we're young. Otherwise, our decisions will potentially haunt us for the rest of our lives.

DECISION-MAKING INVESTMENTS

In chapter 3, you entertained a glimpse of a visit from Future You—twenty years from now. This is the person who ultimately lives with the results of your present-day choices; the person shaped by today's choices you make.

Suppose Future You was able to travel back in time to talk with you right now. What do you think he or she will say to you?

Yes, you need to study hard and floss your teeth; we've covered those things already! Don't you think there's more? Future You might really be interested in how you take care of your body—whether or not you exercise or eat well. After all, he or she ultimately lives with the body you nurture today.

Future You probably cheers when you practice the guitar or piano. He or she might need that skill to ignite the flames of love in the person who becomes Mr. or Mrs. You, and keep those flames burning!

Don't you imagine Future You watches the friends you make, schoolwork you produce, television shows which fill your mind, and hobbies which dominate your time? All of those things matter because they'll affect him or her.

Ultimately, the things you do today shape the person you'll become down the road. You're a great person right now, but you're also becoming someone. Everything you do today influences the person you'll become. You can either help or hurt Future You.

Think about it, a teenager who gets hooked on drugs or alcohol affects more than his or her immediate life. The future self will wrestle with the addiction for years. He or she may lose relationships and jobs, and suffer intense pain until it's brought under control. The decision to start using such substances lasts for years.

It works this way in every arena of life. A teen who grows tired of high school and drops out potentially subjects his or her future self to a life of underpaid jobs and frustrating finances. Meanwhile, the teenager who works hard through school has an opportunity to attend college and work in the field of his or her choice.

A teenager, who racks up debt, spends decades clawing out from under the weight of bills while the teenager, who holds down a job and saves for what he or she buys, is free from such worries. A teenager, who drives recklessly, endangers the lives of people in his or her car, and may be forced to deal with the guilt of injuring a passenger or worse while a conscientious teenage driver is able to sleep well, free from such burdens.

Do you get the point? Our decisions stick with us. This fact isn't just true of teenagers. It applies to everyone. Teenagers, however, are notoriously blind to what I'm telling you. Kids your age often adopt Russell's mantra; they choose to live in the moment, and worry about the future later.

What they don't realize is the future will eventually arrive, and they'll wish like crazy they had been more careful with it. Unfortunately, by then it's too late.

Think about it: the future is like a bank account. Your good decisions are like depositing money into the account. They accrue interest—the more you deposit the more interest you gain. Then, one day when you need money, you find your bank account is plentiful. You have what you need.

Your bad decisions, which are always more expensive than expected, withdraw money from your account. They drain your resources so completely until one day, when you need money, you find the account is empty, and then you have to start all over to rebuild it.

That's how the choices you make right now can affect your future. You're investing in your life—either putting funds into the bank account until one day they pay off, or depleting funds until one day they've disappeared. On that day, Future You will either return from the bank singing your praises, or cursing your name— which is also his or her name, so that's sort of weird!

RIGHT VS. WISE CHOICES

So, since I've attached the reality about your choices in life, you might ask the next natural questions: What are the right choices? How can I ensure I make them? In some instances, the answer is obvious—stealing and murder are wrong. Those choices lead to trouble . . . and more than likely prison!

However, what about subtle choices which aren't obviously sinful or wrong? For instance, how do you decide whether or not to watch a specific show on television, attend a certain party, or even date a certain person. The Bible obviously doesn't give specific instructions about any of these situations, so how do you decide what to do?

In these moments, you have to switch from looking for the right thing to do, to finding the wise thing to do. Look at how Paul explains this dynamic in 1 Corinthians 10:23–24:

> I have the right to do anything, you say—but not everything is beneficial. "I have the right to do anything"—but not everything is constructive. No one should seek their own good, but the good of others.

I want to point out a few things about Paul's instruction. First, notice Paul stressed as Christians, we have a great deal of freedom. The people in Corinth said, "We have the right to do anything," and Paul didn't argue the point.

God doesn't require we live by some strict list of rules and requirements to make Him love us more than He already does. Ephesians mentions we're saved by grace, through faith, not by the things we do (see Ephesians 2:8). So, when we're trying to make one of those tricky decisions, we need to appreciate God has given us freedom with many of them.

However, making good decisions isn't always about what's right and wrong. Go back to the passage referenced in 1 Corinthians—we say, we have the right to do anything, but we need to keep in mind not everything is beneficial.

This literally means, not everything benefits us. Some things are not helpful. Some things are not healthy. Some things flat-out lead to trouble. A wise person looks to the future and avoids such things.

Imagine a little boy preparing to be the ring bearer at his uncle's wedding. Imagine him dressed in a little tuxedo with a black bow tie, and wearing shiny shoes. He has never looked better!

Imagine his mother saying, "Honey, you have thirty minutes before the wedding. I have to go help with a few other things, but I want you to keep your clothes clean. Be careful, and stay off of the playground behind the church. It's muddy back there."

The mother leaves, and the little boy starts to wander around because he is bored and needs to kill some time until the wedding starts. He knows he can't go to the playground, and he wants to obey the rules.

So, he searches for a different place to go. He spots a trail in the woods which leads to a pond. Ponds are interesting. You can skip flat rocks on them, and throw heavy rocks into them. That's fun! Plus, they're full of interesting things like frogs and salamanders.

The little boy eyes the trail, wondering.

Should he . . . ?

Now, I ask you, is walking that path a wise thing for the little boy to do? Remember, his mother only forbade him from going to the playground. She never mentioned this particular path. She never outlawed the pond. So, it must be okay, right?

Of course, we know what'll happen if the boy follows this path. Just walking through the woods is treacherous to his clothes. Not to mention the mud he's sure to find, the briars he's likely to encounter, and the horrible outcome of playing by the edge of the pond in his slick church shoes he is nearly certain to experience!

Can't you see the look on his mother's face? Can't you hear the boy's excuse?

"But Mom, I stayed off of the playground just like you said. You never told me I couldn't play near the pond."

Do you think his mother will be pacified? It wouldn't pacify mine. I can almost hear her voice.

"What were you thinking?"

Now, compare this illustration with the decisions you face. Just like the little boy in the tuxedo, God has given you some instructions while you're in this world.

He said, "Son, I'm going to be back later. Until then, I want you to take care of the people around you, and I want you to try to stay as clean as you can. So, be careful, and here are a few areas to try to stay away from . . . "

That's it. God never micro-manages our lives. He does tell us some places to avoid because He wants us to stay as clean as possible. He does tell us some places to frequent, because He wants us to stay healthy.

Concerning all of the other stuff, He asks us to think through our options and choose paths which lead us to good places. In other words, He wants us to stay out of the mud and pond!

FIND THE RIGHT PATH

How does this look in real life? Let's go back to our examples from earlier. You're trying to decide whether or not to watch a specific show on television. God certainly never specified which shows are acceptable and which shows we must avoid.

As you decide what to watch, there are plenty of things in God's Word to consider: think about who God is and what He values. Think about things God does tell us are sinful.

Does the show I'm considering promote and glorify those things?

Think about the effect the show might have on you. Will it make you want something that's not good for you, think thoughts which might be harmful? Will it make you lie awake at night, scared or bothered, without peace?

If any of these considerations is true, you need to walk away from the television to do something else. Focus on what's wise.

We'll discuss this topic in more detail in the next chapter.

A certain kid in your class is having a party, and he has invited you to attend. The Bible never tells you whose party you can and can't attend, so you step back to study the situation. The people who're invited to this party aren't the people you usually hang out with. These are kids with a reputation for finding trouble. Oh, and your classmate's parents aren't going to be around to supervise the party. You have even heard a rumor someone may sneak in some alcohol.

Seems like a pretty dangerous path, doesn't it? You could definitely reason it's okay to go. After all, you aren't going to do anything crazy. You aren't going to drink alcohol. You're just going for the sake of your friend.

Yet, if you look at the whole situation, you plainly see this path leads to nowhere good, and it'll be hard for anyone who walks it to stay clean. Going to the party may be okay, but it sure isn't wise!

There's a person in your class you sort of like, and you have a feeling the person might like you, too. So, you ask the question: is this a good person to date? Step back and study the situation. You know this person attends a local church, and you have heard the person talk with friends about youth group activities. You also know the person wears a purity ring which represents a pledge to honor God in any dating relationship.

Those things seem positive. Add to it the fact the person is kind to others, conscientious, a hard worker in school, and seems like he or she is a healthy person to be around, not the kind of person who expects you to put him or her ahead of God. On the contrary, the person loves God. The smart decision is seemingly apparent.

I also want to point out a person who doesn't have these traits can be dangerous. That's really the point here. In order to choose the best paths in life, you have to be willing to step back and survey the entire landscape. Think about where these paths lead.

If they lead to trouble, stay away! If they don't, go ahead and walk them. However, always be cautious!

FOLLOW THE GUIDE

One more thing about making good decisions is we live in a dangerous world filled with tricky choices, but God does not expect us to go it alone. On the contrary, God walks the journey with us. How does He do it? Cue another story . . .

Some years ago, a few friends and I decided to try our hand at white-water rafting on a beautiful early-fall day. All of us were excited as we piled into the raft. The four of us settled in with an invited fifth passenger. Actually, we had paid him to come along because none of us had any experience and the river we had chosen presented a pretty big challenge. So, we hired a guide to ride along . . . we were glad we had!

Throughout the day, our guide proved to be invaluable. Not only did he tell us stories and histories of the river that were instructive and entertaining, but he also kept us out of some sticky situations.

For example, late in the trip we came to the outset of a pretty intense rapid, and our guide told us to paddle to the riverbank. When we got there, he explained the best path to navigate this particular rapid. He encouraged us to watch a few rafts try it before we continued.

As we watched, a raft full of people came barreling toward the rapids. The passengers had no guide, and they took no time to think about what they should do. Instead, they blindly charged forward, hit the rapids, and immediately got stuck in a whirlpool. Many people fell out of the raft, and those who held on got drenched with water. As soon as we saw what happened, we followed them.

Guided by our expert, we were able to avoid their mistakes. We hit the rapids perfectly, and even helped recover some of their passengers and belongings. Thank goodness we had a guide riding along with us!

In a way, the situation illustrates how God guides us. He points out places where we should paddle and avoid. As we follow His instructions, we're able to navigate even the toughest stretches of life without crashing.

You might be thinking, *how does God guide me? I can't see Him, so where's His instruction?*

I'm so glad you asked! God guides us through:

- The Bible. This book contains God's complete Word for mankind. In it, He tells us everything we need to know about Him, and about His plan for this world. That's not all. He also filled His Word with practical wisdom to help us make good decisions. He tells us things to avoid and embrace, and also principles pertaining to money, relationships, jobs, friendships, and so many other areas of life. The better we get to know God's instructions through the Bible, the more certain we are to make good life decisions.

- The Holy Spirit. Understanding how the Holy Spirit works can be confusing for anyone, adult or teenager. So, I'm going to resist providing some lofty theological explanation. Instead, just know this: when we become Christians, God sends us a gift. That gift is the Holy Spirit—part of God Himself— who comes to live inside of us. We now have God living in us. The Holy Spirit whispers to our hearts—directing us toward good and right things, nudging us to avoid harmful things. If we remain still and listen to the Spirit's voice inside of us, we'll instinctively make good decisions!

- Other People. Another way God helps us make good decisions is through the influence of other people. This scenario can be tricky because it matters which people have our ears. Think of godly people you know, people grounded in scripture and who seem wise. These people serve as guides just like the river expert in our raft. They can show us things we don't know and can help us find safe paths. However, we have to be willing to listen.

In fact, this is the key to everything—being willing to listen. So often, when people make decisions which cause them to really crash in life, it's because they refused to listen. They ignored God's Word. They ignored the voice inside of them which told them to turn back. They ignored the advice of parents or godly friends who cautioned them to reconsider their path. Instead, they plunged forward and ended up in bad places.

It doesn't have to be this way for you. You'll make mistakes, I understand this. We all make mistakes. You can, however, avoid some big ones if you step back, think, and listen. If you can do this, you'll have so much satisfaction when you look back and see where you've successfully been, and where you're going. Future You will be so proud!

DEVOTIONS: Read Proverbs 27:12. What should you do if you see danger ahead? How does this relate to the decisions you make?

CHAPTER

— 6 —

MANAGING MEDIA

I'VE BEEN SPENDING SOME TIME lately trying to imagine a world without electronic screens. Um, are you still there? You didn't just faint, did you? I know it's a scary concept, but try to be strong. In fact, for just a moment can you be brave enough to imagine with me?

The electronic devices you relish are still relatively new inventions. In fact, if you consider the broader scope of history, television is still a fairly new invention. Your great-grandmother grew up with no television, and even your grandparents can probably remember life without one.

Of course, they all have one now, and watch it every day. Nearly everyone these days spends regular time in front of the television. In fact, these days, it's not just television. We are plugged-in, wired-up, and teched-out in every way possible.

Chances are during the course of any given day, you spend time checking email, updating Facebook, and Googling random phrases. You probably also play Halo on your Xbox, Super Mario Bros. on your Nintendo 3DS, and Angry Birds on your Smartphone.

All the while, you're texting friends, chatting with others, and downloading music which you promptly blast into your ears with an iPod. Oh, and all of that's in addition to watching television which Americans do for an increasing number of hours every day.

Whew! Talk about being plugged in! People living in this culture almost never tune out! Electronic media stays in nearly everyone's ears, which begs the question: What exactly is being pumped into our minds? Do we ever pay attention?

This leads to another question: is there ever a moment when enough is enough, and we tune out, even if only for a little while? After all, our electronics-crazed culture may be harming us more than we think!

MEDIA'S MESSAGE

I still remember the first time my son took an interest in television. He was just a little thing—less than two years old, but he was big enough to run around the house and cause constant chaos. Frankly, his mother and I were exhausted from chasing him.

One day, when we needed some quiet, and he felt especially restless, in desperation I popped a Barney VHS tape into the VCR. In case you don't know what a VHS tape is, ask an adult. Better yet, Google it. I'm sure you'll find a picture on a retro site somewhere! It's what we used back in the Dark Ages of the 1990s.

Anyway, that videotape must have been magic because it cast a spell on my little boy. He glanced at the television screen and froze, mesmerized by the image. Let me phrase it another way: for the first time in his entire life, he was completely still!

For approximately twenty-eight minutes, he stood in front of our coffee table, gripped a plastic hammer mid-air, and watched this strange box he never knew existed. I must confess for his mother and me, those minutes were wonderful!

Honestly, we never felt guilty about letting our children watch television in those days. First, we really did relish those occasional half hour periods of peace and quiet. However, it was more than that. The shows my kids watched taught powerful lessons.

Barney talked about sharing and imagination. Sesame Street taught colors, numbers, and letters. Spot sang about friendship. We closely monitored everything they watched, and the programs supported what we wanted them to learn.

Before you read any further, let's play a game. Take a moment and say aloud what lessons you think television programs for older children and adults teach. If pre-school programs teach about colors, numbers, and how to share toys, then what does Hollywood teach everyone else?

Every story has a lesson. Meaning even when you watch programs for pure entertainment, something is being taught. Can you identify any of the lessons? Say them aloud right now.

The following are a few messages I've seen on television or in movies:

- You're your greatest good. In other words, you need to take care of you before considering anyone else. Do whatever it takes to get ahead, and don't worry about anyone else. They don't matter as much as you do.

- All rules were made to be broken. Right and wrong are simply opinions.

- People are accidents of nature, created apart from God. Meaning they have no purpose or meaning.

- We should all live in the moment. After all, we only live once. Since there's isn't a God and no life after this one, we can live without considering future consequences.
- Sex and revenge are the two highest goals of life.
- All authority should be resisted, especially parental.
- Heaven opens its doors for everyone, no questions asked.
- Love is selfish, temporary, and completely based on emotions.

That was actually a short list compiled from only a few nights of television viewing. I could continue, but you get the point. As sure as Barney stepped onto the screen to teach pre-school lessons back in the day, the characters now on television and radio, and even on gaming systems teach too. The lessons they teach are more subtle and complex, but they are teaching . . . and everyone seems to be listening.

TWELVE YEARS AND COUNTING

How much are we listening? More than we might think. I recently read a study which indicated the average American watches a little over four hours of television each day. This average might not seem like much, but multiply four hours per day times three hundred and sixty-five days per year. This translates into fifteen hundred hours per year.[3]

---

3   David Hinckley, "Americans spend 34 hours a week watching TV, according to Nielsen numbers," by New York Daily News, September 19, 2012, http://www.nydailynews.com/entertainment/tv-movies/americans-spend-34-hours-week-watching-tv-nielsen-numbers-article-1.1162285 (accessed October 3, 2012)

Let the number sink in for a moment. Most Americans watch around fifteen hundred hours of television each year. Let's put the number in perspective. Since each day has twenty-four hours, fifteen hundred hours per year is the equivalent of sixty-two days each year.

Assuming a person lives to be at least seventy-five years old, the person has invested over twelve entire years of his or her life in front of the television . . . twelve years! Can you imagine? This means, if you're in middle school right now, the average person watches television nearly the same amount of time you have been alive!

By the way, those fifteen hundred hours only represent television viewing. They don't factor in the hours people spend surfing the internet, playing video games, listening to music, or staring at their Smartphones.

Can you see how much influence media has on our society?

If not, let me provide one more statistic. Guess how many hours per year you spend in school? Surely, we spend more time there than in front of the television, right? Wrong. You spend about nine hundred hours in school each year. You also (hopefully) spend about two hundred hours in church. Even if you add the two numbers together, they fall short of the time allotted to electronic media.

It's easy to see what wields the most influence on our thinking. Hollywood gets more of our attention than preachers at church and teachers at school, combined.

BE AWARE AND BEWARE!

Is it any wonder our entire culture resembles the art depicted in movies and on television screens? Is it any wonder so many of us embrace the lessons Hollywood teaches?

Every day, we stare at screens of various sizes for hours on end, and in the process, we soak in the view of the life they depict. It only makes sense. Remember, students are spending more time in front of the television than in the classroom at school.

Hollywood knows how much influence they wield. In fact, advertisers count on it. They know when we watch a commercial often enough, we'll memorize its slogan. If I started singing: "Gimme a break, gimme a break. Break me off a piece of that . . . ," I bet most people could finish the catchy jingle without thinking about it.

These jingles, slogans, and images are etched into our memory banks. I sometimes catch myself humming commercial jingles even when I'm not watching television.

The scary thing is it doesn't stop with commercials. We have spent much time watching and listening, and giving these mediums our full attention—we unknowingly soak in more than jingles.

We begin to dress like the characters we watch on television, talk like them, act like them, and even think like them. We laugh at their jokes, even if they're inappropriate. We ignore the language they use, even if it's offensive. We imitate their actions, even when we know they're not making wise decisions.

We do this because it seems these characters have it all together. They always say the right things at the right times. They always look the right way. The guy always gets the girl, and the girl always gets the guy. Everything works out perfectly for them.

There aren't even consequences when they make poor choices. On television, if someone breaks a law, the police look the other way. If a husband or wife is unfaithful to his or her spouse, they'll eventually find fulfillment. Even if someone kills another human being, especially as revenge, they can simply wash their hands and walk away. When the credits roll, everything is wonderful.

That's not real, is it? In the real world, where real people live, life doesn't work that way. In fact, many of the same actors who live perfect television lives struggle mightily off screen.

When they have affairs, their marriages fall apart. When they break the law, they get arrested. Some actually serve time in jail while others are sentenced to perform community service. When they make bad choices, they struggle with guilt and unrest in their lives just like we do. The consequence-free lifestyle they model on television simply doesn't work in real life.

Still, people tune in and pattern their lives after what they see on the screen. How many teenagers have experimented with drugs, alcohol, or pre-marital sex because they saw a beautiful, cool person in a movie who made it look attractive?

How many teens have decided to take the violent acts depicted on television screens or video games to the next level to commit a crime that gets out of hand? How many make life choices which emulate on-screen characters, hoping to find fulfillment.

Fifteen hundred hours of learning per year distorts reality until many people forget how things actually work in the real world. Unfortunately, by the time they remember, the damage has already been done.

SO, WHAT IS THE ANSWER?

Because of the title of this chapter, you might think I'm going to tell you to get rid of your television set, sell your Xbox, and stay away from movie theaters. You can feel it coming, and you're bracing for impact, right?

You can relax. We live in a media-driven culture, and that's not going to change anytime soon. To succeed in this world, we need to be technology-savvy. So, to turn our backs on electronic devices isn't the best idea. Asking everyone to get rid of televisions isn't realistic either.

So, how can we survive the treacherous media onslaught with our faith intact? The following are three things we can do.

UNPLUG (OCCASIONALLY)

All your electronic devices are equipped with a power switch. You remember the button, don't you? It's the one you once used to power-up your device, and it also works in reverse. Forgive my sarcasm, but it sure seems like many of us have forgotten how to power-down these devices.

Our telephones ring and sound off alerts at all hours of the day and night. Our myriad of speakers blast music during every waking hour, even while we are working. Our laptops or tablets stay connected to social media twenty-four hours a day, seven days a week in case someone wants to comment on the picture we posted.

The world of electronic devices never sleeps, and we don't get much sleep either. Have you ever pondered the damage this constant barrage of gadgets is doing us?

Young ladies, imagine there's a guy at school who has caught your eye, and you finally get a chance to go out with him. You imagine an evening of quiet conversation to really find out what he's like.

So, he picks you up for the date and the two of you head to a movie. On the way, he turns the radio to his favorite station. You each sing along with the music.

You get to the theater, choose your seats, and then stare at the movie screen for two hours. Afterwards, you ride to a restaurant with the radio playing, and sit down at a table.

You finally start to talk, but you notice his eyes keep leaving you to focus above your head. When you turn around to see where he is looking, you see a television mounted on the wall showing the big football game.

He tries to pay attention to you, but his eyes are drawn to the screen. Yet, that's okay because your friends keep texting you to ask how the date is going—you feel compelled to answer every text.

Later, he takes you home as the radio continues playing. When you look back on the date, you realize you never got a chance to really talk. You still don't know him. Your only solace is to log onto Facebook and commiserate with your friends.

That's a picture of nearly every minute of every day for many people. Music is constantly playing, the television is regularly broadcasting, and text messages are always arriving. Things are never quiet.

Maybe you like it this way. I understand. Let me suggest, however, to once in a while unplug—take time to collect your thoughts and re-connect with other people and God.

That's why my family has started to choose a day, every once in a while, when we all power down. For one day, we turn the television off, remove the earbuds, silence the telephones, and put away the video games. I know this might sound horrible, cruel, and inhumane—yes, my kids hated the thought, too—but it's actually pretty nice.

On that day, we go for a hike together, ride bikes, throw a Frisbee, or build a campfire and roast marshmallows. On that day, we're able to spend time with each other. We're also able to give our brains time to recoup from the media's toxic connection.

I want to encourage you to try this, too. Unplug yourself from the millions of screens and do something different. I know this might be hard for you to do, but I promise your relationships will grow, your stress-level will lower, and your happiness will intensify. All you have to do is step away from the devices for just a little while!

INFORMED DECISIONS

We acknowledged earlier our technology-savvy culture isn't going to recede. Media will continue to inundate us with programming, music, games, and images. We have a choice about which things we'll embrace. Hollywood creates content, but it can't make us watch, listen to, or play associated mediums. As consumers, we must learn to make informed choices.

So, how do you decide whether or not the movie everyone is going to see is one you should watch? Or whether the popular game is one you should play? The answer to these questions is tricky. After all, everyone is different, and the decision you make for you could be different than the decision your friends make for them.

To make good choices for you, you need to carefully consider what you're putting into your mind. Ask yourself some questions:

- How will watching this program or movie, or playing this game impact me? Will it make me feel unsafe? Will it cause me to lust? Will it make me less sensitive to the real danger of violence, drugs, or harsh language? How will it ultimately affect me?

- Would I be embarrassed if other people I respect and/or trust knew I was watching this program, movie, or video game? For instance, if my mother, teacher, or youth counselor was in the room would I still watch?

- Does watching this program, movie, or video game make me feel guilty, uncomfortable, or dirty? In other words, does it hurt my conscience?

- Could this harm my relationship with God?

If you feel satisfied with the answers, you're probably making a good choice. If the movie, television program, game, or even song you're considering for entertainment doesn't pass the test, find an alternative.

Remember, when you were younger, your parents made these decisions for you. Hopefully, they are still involved in making decisions with you. The older you become, however, the responsibility for making good choices rests increasingly more on you. Think about what you're allowing to access your mind. Set good boundaries and protect your heart.

PLUG INTO TRUTH

Do you know how to identify a counterfeit dollar bill? Counterfeiters make money look so close to the real thing the average person doesn't see the difference until the bank informs them their money is worthless!

Would it surprise you to know experts who identify counterfeit bills don't study counterfeits? Instead, they study the real thing. They learn every tiny detail of genuine currency, and are armed with knowledge, so they're able to recognize fake currency. They have to learn what's true before they can identify what's false.

When it comes to electronic media, we must deal with different kinds of counterfeit truths. I explained to you earlier in this book how Hollywood presents a distorted reality which many people accept as truth. False truth fills the television, movie, and even game system screens to lead many people astray. They can't tell the difference.

Think about the word: truth. It refers to things that are real, constant, and unchangeable. An example is the pattern of stars and constellations. Sailors used to navigate their ships using the stars in the sky to guide them. They knew where the stars were positioned because they had studied them. The stars guided their voyages by what they had learned about them.

That's how it is with God's truth. It's steady and trustworthy, guaranteed to lead us in a good direction. Yet, if we're going to use it to navigate our lives, we have to study it. We need to know it well. We need to read scripture and think about what we're reading. We need to pay attention in church and spend time talking with God about what we learn.

That's the only way to truly overcome the counterfeit reality Hollywood portrays. We can't escape the images or alternative teachings, not completely. We can, however, commit ourselves to study what's true which will help us dissect Hollywood's counterfeit lessons.

In fact, if we ground ourselves in truth, we can actually process the messages from media in a different light. In the midst of the bad lessons we identified earlier, we can also find nuggets of wisdom. Most great stories include examples of heroism, sacrifice, generosity, and kindness. They may be hidden amongst the negative characterizations, but they're still there.

Here's an example: when I was a kid, my parents let me watch the new Superman movie. This was back in the 1980s, so the special effects weren't what they are now. For that time, however, they were pretty exciting. I already knew the story—I had read the comic books. So, when the movie hit theaters, I was ready to watch.

Here's what I wasn't ready for: the use of language. I was a kid and the language in the movie was worse than any I had ever heard. I knew my parents were concerned—they kept exchanging worried looks. We didn't leave the theater, but every time the characters in the movie used profanity, I and my parents cringed. It seemed to me like they were ruining a great story by adding unnecessary language.

It's funny, but looking back I can't really remember the words I heard in the movie theater, but I do remember the story. I remember how selfless Superman was, how he cared for others more than he cared for himself. I remember his courage, and I remember how willing he was to help, even if it cost him.

I left the theater with a better understanding of what it meant to be a hero. I didn't have superpowers, but I could be selfless and courageous, too!

Do you see my point? Even a movie with obvious flaws—in this case language—also had lessons I needed to learn. The trick was I had to hang on to what was right and dismiss the counterfeit.

You can do the same thing with most movies. Even movies filled with counterfeit truths usually include little glimpses of godly qualities. That's because God, our Creator, designed us to appreciate them.

When you tune into your favorite show, find these ideals and celebrate them. Notice the counterfeit ideals, too, and put them out of your mind. Of course, to do this you must know what's true. Once you know for yourself, you can find good lessons even in the midst of counterfeits.

BE ON GUARD

Let's conclude this chapter with a quick reminder. In 1 Peter 5:8, Peter explains the devil prowls around like a roaring lion, looking for someone to devour. In that same verse, Peter gives us advice. He warns us to "be alert and of a sober mind."

Think about the words "be alert." In other words, Peter means to keep our heads up and pay attention. Notice what's happening around us. Don't blindly follow everyone else, but be vigilant. When it comes to media, pay attention to what messages and images we're putting in our minds, and what they're doing to us.

Then, Peter tells us to keep a "sober mind." Sober doesn't mean sad or boring. It means to be serious. If we keep a sober mind, we avoid being swept away by temptations. Instead, we need to focus our eyes on what's right and refuse to become distracted.

So, be alert and of a sober mind. Pay attention to what you're watching, and don't get swept away by the images available. Be strong, and make the tough choices to guard your mind and heart. This might mean missing a certain show your friends all see. Many of them won't understand. In the end, however, you'll find you have something most of them don't: peace, hope, wisdom, and perspective. Who knows, maybe you can point them to a better way, too.

The bottom line is I'm not asking you to toss out your television or tablet. I'm suggesting you recognize this truth: our enemy uses these devices to devour lives.

He steals innocence and muddles thinking. He tempts people by using images of all sorts of unrighteousness. He casts doubt on the living God. He makes wrong seem right, and right seem wrong. He causes us to lose grip on reality.

You can be different. Stand for God. As Paul wrote in 2 Timothy 2, be a person who can stand before God without having to be ashamed, someone who avoids "godless chatter" which spreads so easily, and someone grounded in truth. If you can be this person, God will do great things with and through you. He'll use you in mighty ways to accomplish so much more than a movie character could ever imagine.

DEVOTIONS: Read Proverbs 4:23. How do you think guarding your eyes helps you to guard your heart?

CHAPTER

— 7 —

A LIFE OF MEANING

WHY AM I HERE? WHAT'S THE POINT?

These are life's ultimate questions. I wonder how many people in history have uttered these very words, and then set out on a great journey of self-discovery, hoping to find the answer.

In books, men would often climb mountains, swim oceans, or cross deserts for a hint at the answer to these very questions. In real life, people seem just as desperate.

In previous times, some Native American tribes would send their young men on long, lonely journeys, during which they asked the gods to reveal their life's purpose. Today, people choose different parameters, but they're similar in purpose.

For instance, some people attend college with no direction at all, hoping somehow, during their time there, inspiration will strike. Other people opt to travel the world, or even to work on the mission field until they can figure out the best path for their life. Others simply give up, failing to see any point to life at all. So, they don't even make an effort. They survive day-to-day, but they never try to make an impact.

Do you recognize people like this? As Christians, even though we should recognize the emptiness of these methods, we can all

identify with the questions: Why am I here, Lord? What's my purpose? Why did you put me here on Earth? Where should I go?
What should I do? Does it even matter?

MY WINDING JOURNEY

I remember the first time I asked these questions. I was a senior in
high school, filling out college applications, when I suddenly wondered what I was going to college to learn.

I had planned to be a journalist, to cover sports for a big
newspaper. I wanted to travel the country covering big games,
and maybe be a guest on ESPN's *Sportscenter*. I wanted to make a
name for myself!

Then, the questions came: Is this why God put me on Earth? Is
this my best direction?

These questions rocked my world. I mean, there's obviously
nothing wrong with being a sports reporter. *My life would be boring
without sports!* Yet, I realized I had never asked God if it was where
He wanted me. I needed to ask Him.

So, after pondering for a week, I knelt during a morning church
service, and offered my future to God. I pledged to follow wherever
He led, even if it wasn't what I had planned.

God didn't give me firm, concrete answers that day. In fact,
since that very moment, my life has been filled with unexpected
turns. Every time I think I have things mapped out, He opens a
new door and I change direction again. Life with Him is more
exciting than anything I could've imagined for myself! I tell you
my story to show you how quickly things change when you walk
with God.

Right now, you may have a plan for the rest of your life. You may already know the career you want, the town you want to live, and even the person you want to marry! Who knows, maybe these things will happen just the way you've planned.

Just remember to invite God into your planning. After all, if you want to live a life with meaning and purpose, you need to follow His lead.

Others may read this book and think, *how do I know what I want to do in the future? I'm just in middle school. I have plenty of time to decide!*

That's so true! However, it can't hurt to spend a few minutes thinking about the future, and God's purpose for your life.

The rest of this chapter is designed to do just that—to help you spend a few minutes thinking about why you're here, why it matters, and what you need to know right now. We're going to explore these questions by considering three important truths.

TRUTH NO. 1:
GOD CREATED YOU WITH PURPOSE

I don't know if you ever spend time reading the book of Psalms. The psalms are somewhat tough to read unless you're into poetry. However, you should give them a try. They convey some pretty incredible ideals.

For instance, read this excerpt from Psalm 139. It communicates something you really need to know:

> For you created my inmost being;
>> you knit me together in my mother's womb.
> [14] I praise you because I am fearfully and wonderfully made;

your works are wonderful,

I know that full well.

¹⁵ My frame was not hidden from you

when I was made in the secret place,

when I was woven together in the depths of the earth.

¹⁶ Your eyes saw my unformed body;

all the days ordained for me were written in your book

before one of them came to be.

Were you able to read thoroughly through the verses? What do they tell you? I want you to notice the following things.

First, notice God created you (vv. 13–14). You didn't appear by accident; God created you. In fact, He knitted you together in your mother's womb. What an incredible image!

Today, many people seemingly accept the idea we were created by accident, by chance. They assume we're nothing more than the product of some arbitrary, scientific phenomenon—an amoeba which became a lizard, and then became a monkey which became you.

Okay, I oversimplified, but that's the spirit of their argument.

So, according to this assumption, we're a random act of nature. As a result, we have no designer, and life has no meaning. What a bleak thought!

However, thank God He tells us in His Word He created us.

Secondly, notice God has a purpose us (v. 16). Before we were even born, God knew everything we'd accomplish. He knew our strengths and weaknesses, our successes and failures, and our best and worst moments. He saw everything we'd become.

Think about that. God created us for a reason. The first reason is so we can get to know and love Him. We're His kids.

Yet, there's another reason, too. God wants us to work for Him. He wants us to use our time and the resources He has given us to accomplish things. He gives us talents, gifts, and opportunities, and He wants us to learn to use them for Him.

At this point, you might think, *what does that have to do with me? I'm still a kid.*

You're right, but even now you have opportunities to make an impact for God. In fact, you're making a difference in the world right now whether or not you know it. Right now, today, you're planting seeds in the soil of this world. One day, those seeds will turn into something.

TRUTH NO. 2: EVERYONE SOWS AND REAPS

You're probably already familiar with the concept of sowing and reaping. Depending on where you live, you probably see it in action through nature every year.

At my house, in May, my wife puts on her garden clothes and calls everyone out to the garden. We spend hours planting little seeds in straight rows, and then covering them with dirt. It's pretty amazing how the little seeds grow into plants which provide so much food for our family.

Bible scribes often compare our decisions, words, and actions to sowing seeds. They compare the things we do, words we say, ways we choose to spend our time, and things to which we put in our minds to little seeds being planted in the dirt. Over time the seeds grow into something larger and produce fruit.

If we plant good, healthy, and righteous things, then good things grow. If we fill our soil with bad decisions, words, and actions, bitter fruit grows. Either way, we're always sowing seeds.

Allow me to dwell for a moment on this point. When we plant seeds in the garden at my house, my wife always marks the rows to remind us what we planted. If we plant black-eyed peas in one row, we can count on the fact black-eyed pea plants will grow. If we plant corn seeds, we know corn will grow. The type of seed planted determines the type of plant growth.

You're probably thinking, *Duh, everyone knows this!*

However, when it comes to life, many of us forget this principle. We forget how the seeds we plant impact other people.

For instance, how do you talk to the other kids at your school? Are you cruel? Do you gossip? Do you cut other people down?

Our words are like tiny seeds that grow in other people's lives. Unfortunately, the fruit they produce can be poisonous.

If we use words filled with love, encouragement, and kindness, those seeds grow. They have the power to change someone's life for the better.

Another way we plant seeds in life is through the things God has given us? Are you generous with your stuff? Do you share with people who don't have as much as you? Are you willing to give even when it hurts?

When you give, you sow seeds which grow into something larger. Sometimes, the fruit which comes from those seeds changes people's lives. They experience joy and peace because of your generosity. However, when you plant seeds of selfishness, the resulting fruit growth brings bitterness.

Do you see how this works? God created you with a purpose, and He wants you to use your time to plant lasting things to show other people His love. You don't have to be rich, popular, or talented to do this. On the contrary, one little seed can do more than you think. We always reap more than we sow!

Last summer, my wife planted maybe fifty green bean seeds, but we harvested way more than fifty green beans. We planted thirty tomato plants, but we harvested hundreds of tomatoes. That's because in the garden—and in life—we always reap more than we sow.

When people forget this principle and plant unhealthy seeds in the soil of their lives, they find the consequences last much longer than they expected. Those seeds keep producing fruit. Of course, the opposite is true, too.

You have the potential, right now, to put things in your life to help you forever! That's why it's so important for you to ponder what seeds you're planting in your life right now.

What can you plant now which can help you later? What habits, skills, and knowledge can you nurture while you're young, which will reap a harvest when you're older? It's not too early to think about what's growing in your life.

TRUTH NO. 3: THE WORLD IS BIGGER THAN YOU

This is the final truth I want to share with you, and it's a big one. Many of your friends haven't learned this, yet. Many adults have forgotten it . . . if they ever knew it.

This truth is the foundation of successful lives. It's so simple, yet so difficult to grasp. Here it is: the world doesn't revolve around you.

It's a simple sentence, but such a profound and important concept. You're not the center of existence. People aren't here to please you. Government isn't designed to serve you. God doesn't exist to grant your every desire.

Don't misunderstand, you're an important person, created by God with unique and precious abilities. Yet, you were created to serve Him, not the other way around.

Ponder this revelation for a moment. Let it sink in. Then, take it a step further.

This world is bigger than you, and there are important principles and causes which require your attention, dedication, and even sacrifice. In fact, I'll phrase it another way: there are things in life worth dying for.

If what I just wrote made you catch your breath, that's good. I didn't type the words easily, and I wouldn't expect you to regard them lightly. Instead, I want to help you understand my admonition.

Have you ever visited Arlington National Cemetery? If not, have you ever seen pictures of the historic cemetery? Its hallowed grounds are beautiful. Obviously, someone has put incredible effort to ensure it look nice, and for good reason.

Underneath the 624 acres of land in Arlington National Cemetery rests the remains of more than four hundred thousand American war veterans from the American Revolution to Iraq and

Afghanistan.[4] Over four hundred thousand headstones, each one represents a different name, each name represents a different story. However, the end of each story is the same; someone was willing to sacrifice his or her life for America's greater good as a nation.

These soldiers' sacrifices beg the question: why? What motivates people to give everything? Here's the simplified answer: they recognized a higher ideal. They lived for a higher calling, a greater good, something outside of themselves. They loved people and their country so much they fought to keep them free. They were willing to pay any price.

I really want you to understand this concept: some things in life are just that important. They're bigger than you. Your job is to figure out what those things are, and then live your life for them.

It may not mean you must literally sacrifice your life for those things. I hope you never have to be in such a position. However, when you find something bigger than you, don't hold anything back. This is the key to seizing a life of meaning.

Pause for a moment to think through this revelation. Even at your age, I bet you can identify some things in life which are more important than any of us.

For me, my relationship with God is at the top of the list. Wherever He leads, I'm willing to follow. My family is up there, too. You had better believe I would give my life for them if needed. In a way I do—I work hard every day to provide for their needs.

My country is on the list. I've never been in the military, but if Uncle Sam needs me to protect our freedoms, I'll answer the call.

---

4   Arlington National Cemetery, "About Arlington National Cemetery," Arlington National Cemetery, http://www.arlingtoncemetery.mil/AboutUs/Default.aspx (accessed October 1, 2012)

Each of these things is bigger than me, and I pledge allegiance to them. What's on your list? I feel sure you can name things in your life deemed that important if you just give it some thought.

You need to know many people don't live that way. In fact, many people live their lives completely opposite of what I just described. They make it their life goal to look out for number one—themselves.

They make money, store it away, and pile up treasures they never use or share. They give only when it's convenient, serve only when it helps them somehow, and only love those who love them back. For such people, sacrifice is a foreign concept. Their entire lives are about building for themselves.

Let me tell you a secret about these type of people—they have no real joy. The reward for all of their treasures and conquests is a hunger for more. They're never satisfied or content. Life is nothing more than an empty pursuit to gain more. Then, when they reach the end of life, they look at the value of what they've collected, and discover they're left with nothing. They can't take what they've accumulated with them.

I implore you to avoid the emptiness of this path. The world is bigger than you, and that's a good thing! You're part of something grand, and your life really does matter.

By the way, this means people looking for the meaning of life have an answer. The meaning of life is to remember there's a God who created you. He wants you to make a difference in His name.

You can start by remembering even your smallest action can produce a great harvest. Then, find the things in life which matter most and start planting seeds.

At this moment, your whole life is stretched out in front of you, so start thinking about how to use it. Make an impact today, and ask God to show you how to use your talents in the future. He'll answer your prayer.

Just consider yourself warned. You're in for an exciting adventure!

DEVOTIONS: Read Ephesians 2:10. What do you learn about your life from this verse?

For more information about
Matthew Sink
&
A Map for the Middle
please visit:

Email: matthewsink@pinedale.org
Twitter: twitter.com/MatthewSink
Facebook: www.facebook.com/mapforthemiddle
Blog: pcchighroad.wordpress.com

....

For more information about
AMBASSADOR INTERNATIONAL
please visit:

www.ambassador-international.com
@AmbassadorIntl
www.facebook.com/AmbassadorIntl